CONNECTING THE DOTS

Facing Pain, Finding Peace

By
Scott Ranck

PublishAmerica
Baltimore

First printing

At the specific preference of the author, PublishAmerica allowed this work to remain exactly as the author intended, verbatim, without editorial input.

Unless otherwise indicated, all Scripture quotations are taken from the Holy Bible, New Living Translation, copyright © 1996. Used by permission of Tyndale House Publishers, Inc., Wheaton, Illinois 60189. All rights reserved.

ISBN: 1-4241-7756-1
PUBLISHED BY PUBLISHAMERICA, LLLP
www.publishamerica.com
Baltimore

Printed in the United States of America

Dedication

To Gayle, the love of my life;
My spiritual adventure partner

Acknowledgments

I am so grateful for many people who have shaped my thinking. This writing is a conglomeration of things I have learned from many sources, gathered, lived, filtered and attempt to put together in a way that makes sense. First, I am grateful for a vital relationship with Jesus Christ. His gentle teaching, and showing me Himself and myself, is the core of everything. Next, I am so grateful for my wife, Gayle, who has taught me so much while loving and accepting me unconditionally. My best friend, Willie Pegram, first introduced me to recovery. Willie was the first person I told everything to, my deepest, darkest secrets. After hearing the worst about me, he hugged me and told me he loved me and he was proud to have me as his pastor! Pastor Jimmy Acree who has been a great support through all my battles. Thanks to David Ferguson, Peter Scazzero, Daniel Goleman, John Eldredge and Lance Dodds, all who stretched me through their teachings and writings. The men of Bay Life Church in Brandon, Florida have given me the opportunity to flesh out these concepts. Finally, thanks to my sister, Michelle Koons, for editing the text and giving me valuable feedback.

Scott Ranck, March 2007

Contents

Introduction

I was a senior pastor for eighteen years. I had a degree in theology. I had transitioned a declining traditional church into a growing vibrant church. I had built a staff that had been together many years. I had led many people to the Lord and taught many how to have healthy marriages, how to handle their finances, how to discover their own gifts and use them to help others. I had a sense of God's favor on my life. I knew the Bible fairly well and had a daily time with the Lord. I was able to stand before hundreds of people every week and passionately teach a message from the Bible that related to every day life. I also had an aggravating battle against a dark side. That battle seemed to never leave me for very long. On occasion, in times of extreme pressure or boredom I would yield to the temptation. I quickly would confess my sin to God and ask for strength never to do it again but often the battle would become stronger, requiring a lot of energy to fight it. There were times of relief that I felt I was "cured." Those times of success often lasted for some time but then the war raged back to life again.

I am a student by nature, very inquisitive and was always looking for an answer to my dilemma. How could I be a Christian, even a pastor and still be battling with this thing I brought from adolescence? I talked to other pastors and many had the same battle. I read everything I could find but nothing seemed to help. My battle was with what my confidants and I called, "the beast." It was the battle with lust. It showed its ugly head in many ways but one of the most predominant ways was through the lure of pornography.

I have come to believe all human beings run to something. There are no exceptions! So, even if your battle is not with lust, do not put this book down because, I believe you will gain insights into your own struggle as I unfold my discoveries throughout these chapters. I believe that when you belong to the Lord, He will use everything life throws at you to teach you. The world is His classroom. He uses the good, the bad and the ugly to shape us. He will never lead you to sin, but He will use your wrong choices to teach you, if you are open.

You may be growing tired. You put on a good front at church but you know you are losing the battle on the inside. There was a time in my life I would have never believed I could be as free as I am today. Unfortunately, I crossed so many lines; in the end, it cost me my role as the lead pastor. My choices took me down to a place where I was not sure, I could go on or if I wanted to go on. I nearly lost everything valuable in my life. However, at the lowest point...I will tell you that story later. Go with me through these pages. It is my life, but my guess is you will see yourself and your struggle as well. I invite you to join me for the journey.

Chapter One
WHAT A BABY!

Most newborn babies are not that attractive! They have just come through a very traumatic experience. I remember our own babies being red, puffy, and even bruised after delivery. I remember telling my wife after the birth of one of our children, "The baby looks like a boxer who lost the fight!" So, as a pastor who made it a practice of visiting the newborns, I had many occasions to attempt to say something kind when looking at someone's newborn bundle. Sometimes all I could say honestly was, "What a baby!"

Did you ever get to see any home movies of the day your parents brought you home from the hospital? I'm from an era where the old black and white 8mm movie camera was a new creation. I do remember seeing the home movies of all three of the kids that grew up at my parent's house. When my mom and dad brought those little bundles home, guess what they were? My older sister, younger brother, me and every other human being who was ever born on planet earth were a bundle of needs. It does not matter if you were born into a two-parent family, a single parent home, or if you were adopted. Remember seeing the Romanian orphanages, in the 1990's? The little children packed in a room of cribs? Babies only a year or so old who would sit in the crib holding themselves while rocking themselves for comfort. All of us were born with the same need for comfort. All of us were born with a need to be loved, valued, protected, and fed. All of us were born with a need for shelter, for nurture, for direction in life. Any baby born and then just left to take care of her self will soon die. All of us were created to have our needs met by others in our lives.

The experts tell us that each of us needs our mother's love and our father's approval but that just scrapes the surface. Every human has emotional needs, physical needs and spiritual needs. These needs are universal. All people of all cultures of all ages have the same basic needs.

I want you to pause and reflect for a few minutes. I want you to imagine your mother giving you birth. Happy Birthday, you have arrived! Imagine from that point on you could go back and control how everyone treated you throughout your entire childhood development. What would that childhood look like to you?

I want to do this exercise on paper for you. Feel free to edit or insert your own dreams and desires of what you would have liked your growing up experience to look like.

I would wave the wand over my mom and dad requiring them to love each other deeply and be at peace. In those first days and weeks, I would want to know I was really loved and wanted. I would want to be held very close and talked to. I would want my parents to be proud of me and show me to all their friends as if I was a special gift to them. It would be great for both parents to be so much in tune with me that they could discern my noises, cries and coos so that every real need would be met, yet without spoiling me. As I grew, I would still want both parents active with me. Regularly expressing their love for me, taking care of all the needs that I could not yet do for myself, while very patiently teaching me what I could do for myself. I would want to be held close at times and read to, and talked to. I would want to be looked in the eye and told what a special gift from God I am.

As I grew, I would want my dad to pay attention to me and teach me things and do stuff with me. Since I am a guy, I would want dad to do fun and daring stuff with me. Rough and tumbling on the floor, teaching me to play some sports and really enjoying hanging out with me. I would want him to show me his tools and other manly stuff. He would take me fishing or camping. Dad would teach me about creation. He would introduce me to adventure and excitement in a wholesome way. I would want to hear his stories of growing up. I would want to know everything he could tell about his childhood. I would want to help him work and fix stuff. It would be awesome to get to go to work with him one day.

My mom would read to me and love on me. I would want her

to tell me what a great man my dad is and to share her dreams for me. She would share with me what it was like for her growing up. I would want her to let me explore and be a boy and yet at times baby me.

I would always want to know home was a safe place. Home would be a place where both mom and dad could be trusted with anything. Where direction and correction would be given when needed, but always with the foundation of knowing I am loved and accepted. Always knowing they believed in me and felt God had a special purpose for my life.

I would want to know, as I got older, that choices always have consequences and that mom and dad loved me so much they would let me feel the consequences of my choices. I would want them to give me the freedom to make many of my own choices but always with the realization, I would have to deal with the results one way or the other. Again, always knowing they were there, never wavering in their belief in me, never ever questioning whether I was loved.

My parents would be people who had a real relationship with God. They would admit when they were wrong. They would be clear on what their purpose in life is. They would teach me to talk to God, to trust Him and to make living for Him my top priority. They would teach me His values and how to have compassion for people. They would help me make sense of tragedy. They would teach me why God put some fences around our lives to protect us. They would teach me what a special gift I was to them from God and that I belonged to God. They would love me so much that when I hurt they would hurt, when I was happy they would want to share in it. When I succeeded, they would burst with pride. When I failed they would reassure me of their love and show me how everything was an opportunity to grow.

Finally, as I grew to young adulthood and moved from under their roof, the foundation of my life would be established. I would have grown to be comfortable in my own skin. I would have an internal set of values I caught from them. I would know that no matter what, their love and support was still present. Their role now has shifted to friend and confidant. There is now a sense of accomplishment on their part and a mutual respect between us.

Your story and desires may be slightly different from mine. However, my guess is that my feelings are pretty much universal. What adult, no matter their age, could look back and have wished for less? No matter how well your parents did, they too, are less than perfect. Most do the best they can with what they have to work with at that stage of their lives. However, for most of us looking back over our childhood, we will see glaring gaps between what we wish our childhood experience had been and what in reality it was. **Every one of those gaps represents some need that went unmet.** As we will see in the next chapter, those unmet needs whether large or small, create pain.

Chapter Two
UNMET NEEDS = PAIN

I remember being in a church when our children were very small. The hall was crowded with noisy people as the group transitioned from one room to another. Over all the commotion, I heard one of my daughters crying and I instantly moved to action. Some lady, who was not a parent, asked where I was going. I said, "I heard my daughter crying and want to see if she is all right." The lady was amazed I could discern my daughter's cry through all the other noise.

From our earliest memories, we associate a baby's cry with some need that is unmet. It may be a full diaper that has been ignored too long, or an empty belly that needs filled or it may just be a need to be sure you are there. It may be a cry to say, "I just want to be held close and made to feel secure."

Whatever the need is that currently isn't being met provokes crying from the baby. **Unmet needs equal pain.**

I remember, as if it were yesterday, one Saturday morning when I was about eight years old. Dad was home from work, which always gave me a little hope that he would do something with me, though that hope was usually not realized. This day proved to be no different. I knew Dad was getting ready to do something or go somewhere. He began getting some things together. He went to the garage and got his fishing pole and some other fishing equipment. My boyhood fantasies were springing to life. Could it be? Soon a car pulled up alongside our house. It had a couple guys in it who were friends of my dad. He never told me where he was going; he hugged my mom, and messed up my hair and went out the gate, never saying much of anything to me. I stood at the gate looking through with anticipation, hoping he might look back, see me, and decide to take me with him. Instead, he had gotten in the car and never looked back. He was already laughing and joking with the other men. The car, with boat in tow, pulled away and I stood there shattered. I needed my father's approval. I needed him to communicate how much he loved me by including me. The unmet need **represented** here, the need for dad's approval, created a pain in my life that would take years to uncover and heal. The need was to have an engaged father who believed in me and convinced me I had what it took to become a man.

For some of you, not being included on a fishing trip seems like a minimal hurt compared to what you faced. The story is used as one illustration of how much a boy longs for connection with his dad. For many, it is more than just no connection. I know people whose fathers beat them or sexually abused them. I can only imagine the pain that created.

The point is **all unmet needs create pain**. The pain may differ in severity and depth but pain is pain. As you think about this concept early in the book, allow yourself to look back. Let me caution you here. As you look back, it is for **one purpose and that is not to blame someone else for your current situation**. Rather, the reason I want you to look back and identify some early times that you remember needs not being met and pain being inflicted, is those are areas of woundedness that often contribute to some of your unhealthy or unwanted behaviors and attitudes in the present. That is why I have titled this book, *Connecting the Dots*. As you continue through this book, I believe you will better understand yourself at a deeper level. It will help you make sense out of the current struggles.

Imagine growing up in an environment where there did not seem to be any adults around to steer you, help you or care for you. One lady told me how in her very early years both her parents worked, she would get up in the morning for first grade, and no one was around. She dressed herself, fixed her hair, got any breakfast she could find and then walked to school by herself. She told me that on rainy days, she would come out of school and watch the other kids being picked up in front of the school by parents and she would wait with a hope someone might come to get her, but it never happened. The schoolyard would be empty when she would head for home, walking alone in the rain. When she got home there was no one there to welcome her. There are so many unmet needs in that story that it hurts me to write it, let alone imagine the depth of woundedness that little girl experienced.

It would be naïve to think that kind of early life experiences do not leave any marks. I can easily see that little girl growing up to feel she must not be worthy of being loved. I can see where that cavernous gaping wound for attention and feeling unlovable could easily be exploited.

A high school guidance counselor told me the above-described pattern is fast becoming the norm. He said numbers of students reported to him they have no meals together as a family in the course of a week.

You have your own story. The only crucial thing I want you to grasp, as we start connecting the dots, is **all unmet needs you experience, regardless of your age, create pain.**

The amazing thing to me is this pain is not only inflicted when we are little. One year at Thanksgiving, our family had moved to a new state and was not going to make it home. Instead of sitting home feeling lonely we decided we would go to a nursing home and see if we could find someone who had no family to visit them. Our family actually prayed about it and asked God to lead us to someone who could use the encouragement. We found a home, went in, and told the people at the information area what we hoped to do. They gave us the name of a lady who they felt fit the situation. Our family went in to this elderly, bedfast woman's room. We told her we prayed that morning for someone to encourage and she was where we ended up. She began to have some tears roll down her checks as she told us she also had prayed that morning and ask God not to let her spend Thanksgiving all alone. She had a need to experience love and care and to have "family" around for a holiday. The meeting of the need brought a great level of joy for her and fun for us too. Both our family and the elderly lady felt like God cared about us and heard our prayers. What if no one ever showed up to see her that day? I rest my case. **Unmet needs always create pain, no matter what age.**

Unfortunately, that is not the only source of pain in our lives. We have the innate ability to inflict serious pain on ourselves, and we will look at that over the next two chapters as we continue to connect the dots.

Chapter Three
BORN WITH A BENT

There are many views on how we come into this world. Are we born as blank slates and then shaped by our upbringing, the environment and our education? Are we born good, and then it is only the mess around that corrupts us? My approach in this book is the biblical view of humanity. You and I have come into this world with a bent toward self-centeredness and a desire to do what we want to do. In our native selves, we do not like authority telling us how to behave or what to touch or not touch. Therefore, as soon as we are old enough to make some choices, we choose some things that will hurt us.

I remember when our son was heading into the age many refer to as "the terrible twos." It is during that time of childhood development when children are learning to use the word "no." They begin to take their first steps of independence and want to test and sometimes challenge all the boundaries. Anyway, we had a CD player on a stand that was within his reach. He clearly knew the knobs were off limits. One day in a battle of wills, I was on the floor near the CD player and Tim was eyeing it very closely. His little hand began to extend out toward the knob. He and I locked eyes as his hand defiantly kept inching closer to the knob all the while he was staring me down. I finally said, "No," very firmly, and his steely gaze turned to a loud cry.

All of us seem to have an innate desire for some forbidden fruit. It is deep within all of us. The Bible refers to it as our sinful nature. There are no exceptions to this flaw and it always reveals itself in the choices we make. Don't take me wrong here, we all make some really good choices too. But, everyone reading this book knows there have been times when you knew something was wrong, and would be hurtful to you and others, but you chose to do it anyhow, just because you wanted to!

I look back on my junior high school days, at some of the things I did, and wonder what would possess me to do those things. There was a boy in our school, who was mentally handicapped and his head was very big. Some of us kids almost seemed to thrive on this poor kid's weakness. I remember calling him ugly names and he being so hurt and angry he would be crying while chasing me around the school parking lot. Why was I so cruel? I was not raised that way. Where does that ugly side of us come from? Why is it that, as soon as we learn there is a line drawn, we want to cross it?

A friend of mine told me a story that as a young man his father had bought a brand new car. One night late, he and his friends decided they would climb out their windows and take the new car for a ride. They were having the time of their lives, out riding around in the car. They had decided they needed to get home, go back to bed, and call it a night. On the way home, they went through a low-lying area that had filled with run-off water. They thought they could make it, but the water was deeper than expected and the engine actually went under water, sucked the water into the engine, and killed it.

They had the car towed to a shop, and the next morning when the boy's dad got up and wondered where his brand new car was, his son told him the story. The dad went to the shop and found out the car had major damage. He went back home and never yelled at the boy. He simply handed the keys and payment book to him and said, "Congratulations. son, you just bought a brand new car." It took the boy years to pay for it!

Guess what? It does not matter if you are two, twelve, twenty-two or ninety-two; you and I still have that bent toward doing things our own way. No one reading this can say, "I've never made a wrong choice."

I'm writing from a biblical value system. What that means in the case of sexuality is that God has put a fence around sexual behavior. All sexual relationships outside of the commitment of marriage are out of bounds (Hebrews 13:4). The reason for this is the high emotional, spiritual and physical price tag that comes with sexual union outside of a lifetime commitment. Have you seen on the news lately that one of the groups with the fastest spread of STDs (sexually transmitted diseases) is senior citizens?

Senior adults, many who believe it is morally wrong for them to engage in such behavior outside of marriage, do it anyway.

My guess is, many of you reading this right now can point to at least one really hurtful choice you have made, that violated every thing you believe in. You may not even be sure why you did what you did, but you chose to do it anyway. Let me assure you, you are in good company. The apostle Paul says in a classic passage in Romans 7:15ff that he found himself doing things he did not want to do, but he did them anyway!

If you have made it into your twenties, you could probably write a short book of your own just on all the poor and sometimes downright sinful choices you have made already.

Here is what I want you to know from this chapter, as we head into the next, **both the unmet needs you experience and the wrong choices you make produce pain**. Let's look at several kinds of self-inflicted pain that is the result of those hurtful choices!

Chapter Four
WRONG CHOICES = PAIN

Someone said, "Conscience isn't the red light to stop poor choices, it is the blue light flashing after the choice is made." Billy Graham is credited with saying, "If people could accept God's forgiveness and really feel it, most mental health hospitals would be releasing their patients." After committing adultery with Bathsheba, King David wrote in Psalm 32 about the state of his mental health. He talked about his inability to sleep and how his bones roared all day long. His spirit had dried up. The emotional pain was overwhelming. When he attempted to sweep his junk under the carpet, it nearly killed him mentally and emotionally. When he was willing to confess his sin relief came.

There are some obvious internal pains that our hurtful choices cause. Guilt is the most obvious. Feeling guilty is a terrible feeling! When I feel guilty, I am not able to fully engage with others. There is a sense I am hiding something. That hiding can often lead to withdrawing from certain key relationships. This isolation leads to loneliness, which is also painful. The next thing I know, I am in full-blown depression. I may mope around for days, blaming everyone else for my sour mood, before I connect the dots and realize it all started with a wrong choice that I made.

Often, these consequential painful feelings drive us to make other poor choices to numb the new feelings that resulted from our original hurtful choice. This cycle can become a terrible downward spiral. It often leads one into the addictive cycle of pain, medicate, new pain, and medicate again.

The human family is stubborn! Often I have lived with secret wrong choices for years. There was a time when I confessed to God, but never to a human. Many things done in the teen years have been kept locked away in some secret compartment. As we grow up and continue to make poor choices, it appears we are getting away free. We often think, "I can do this and nothing negative is happening, so why not continue?" Recently, I have become aware that God not doing anything is not a sign of His approval. It is simply what Peter says in the Scriptures, "God is not willing that any of us perish but He is very patient toward us wanting us all to come to repentance." (2 Peter 3:9) The window of time given to us to change our hurtful choices and behaviors is a grace gift. It is a chance to find the resources to change destructive behaviors before we crash and burn. God allows us to humble ourselves rather than being humiliated by exposure of our secrets to others. The illusion that we can manage our sin and maintain the rest of our lives, seduce us to think we will never be found out.

The pain that hurts the most for me, is a feeling that God is very distant, and I am on the outside looking in. If you have ever known a time of intimacy with God, a time when He was teaching you things about Himself and yourself. If you have ever known what it felt like to know He was using you, to lose that closeness due to violating some boundary, is, to me, the greatest pain. The feeling of being dead inside while alive outside is a terrible place to live.

Several years ago, I really blew it big time. At the time, I had been the lead pastor of a growing church for eight years and had been a pastor for fifteen years. Over those years, especially when I was in a situation I did not know how to handle, I escaped through some attempt at lustful behaviors. Most of what I have learned and I am writing about came through the humiliation of where that pattern led. I did not fully understand how that sin had softened my defenses against other "outside the boundary" choices.

Through a whole series of things I will not go into here, I had confessed to my wife and our elders to my inappropriate behavior. I confessed at the time because I felt the noose tightening. My wife had sensed my distance and confronted me with her concern. I admitted to her I had been leaning on someone else for emotional support. I shared the story with our elders and they decided to send me to a retreat center for counseling wounded pastors. The guilt of my wrong, the secrets

I was keeping, and the tightrope walk of what to reveal and still save my marriage and my career became very tedious. Before I left for the counseling center, my best friend and I went to breakfast. He looked into my eyes and asked me, "Where are you? I look into your eyes but you are not in there. I wonder if some aliens have abducted you!"

That pain of disconnecting from God, from my wife and even from myself is the greatest self-inflicted pain I know. Living with secrets, especially secrets that violate what I claim to believe, is especially destructive. Maybe that is why Romans 14:23 teaches us even if we think something may be wrong and we choose to do it anyway, for us it is wrong. We violated our own self-integrity.

Over these first four chapters, we are discovering that our **unmet needs cause pain** but our bent toward wrong and the **wrong choices we make also create pain.**

Throughout our life experience there is one more source of pain we all experience. We'll consider that next, in Chapter Five.

Chapter Five
LIFE HURTS

I'll never forget the night. It was a rainy Friday. Our family was at the dinner table when the phone rang. I can still see my mom as she answered the phone and reacted strongly to the message she heard. She hung up the phone, dropped her head, and began to weep. I was only a fifth grader at the time and really had not faced any tragedy in life. My dad asked her what was wrong and mom said, "Shirley committed suicide." Shirley was my aunt, my favorite uncle's wife. She was only twenty-eight years old. I remember being taken out of school one day to go by the funeral home and view my aunt's body. It was a lot for an eleven year old to understand.

Unfortunately, that wasn't the end of my learning that life hurts. Our family like all families has had its share of suffering. Fast-forward, I'm now twenty years old and married to Gayle. We are living in our first home. This time it was a Sunday morning about 6:30am, when the phone rang. I answered and it was my dad. He said he had some terrible news and didn't want us to see it on TV before he could tell us. There was a car wreck. A drunk driver killed two of my aunts and an uncle, and another uncle was in critical condition. Our family was close, and one of the couples was almost like a second set of parents to me growing up. I lived directly across the street from them and had to go over and take care of the house for them while my uncle recovered. It was unbelievable to walk into the funeral home and see three caskets lined up head to toe across the room.

One of my greatest personal blows has been the death of my dad. He and mom had come to visit our family on their way from Pennsylvania to Florida. We lived in North Carolina at the time. On their way home, they stopped again. Dad was not feeling very well, complaining of a stiff neck and some digestion issues. Upon arriving home, he became violently ill. Within a couple days, he was diagnosed with a brain tumor. Following brain surgery we were told he would only live six weeks to three months. The time estimate was accurate and he left us July 4th, early in the morning. Our family had spent the last ten days of his life at his side helping to care for him. I had the honor of preaching his funeral. Thankfully, we had no unfinished business between us. I've found the relational wounds before death often cause the greatest sting after death. I had no regrets or ill feelings toward him. You can read about how our relationship was healed in Appendix A.

No one goes through life without being hurt. Whether it is through the death of a loved one, the break up of a relationship, a betrayal, financial hardship, going off to war or loss of health, all of us experience life hurts. Most of us move into some kind of survival mode when those hurts come our way.

I remember talking to another man who lost his father. Upon the death of his dad, the man said he went outside and weeded his father's flowerbeds like a wild man. In his grief, he felt like he needed to do something. As a pastor, I was with many people in their times of loss and sorrow. I've seen people who would publicly proclaim the evils of alcohol, but have a secret bottle next to their bed so they could sleep at night. I've watched others engage in so many outside activities they barely had time to relax in between. Others could not stand to be alone; their homes were noisy places with televisions and radios playing in every room, in an attempt to drown out the awful noise of silence. Others still would isolate themselves from everyone, withdrawing into their own closed-off world, hiding like a wounded animal.

Life, then, is really all about navigating through all this pain coming at us from these three primary sources. Our unmet needs, our own hurtful choices and the painful things life just throws our way. Universally, humans do not do well with all this pain.

There is a very normal response to all of it, and we will begin to investigate that response next in Chapter Six. Then, we are going to regress in chapters seven and eight to examine pain more closely.

Chapter Six
TAKE TWO ASPIRIN—
THE NORMAL HUMAN
RESPONSE TO PAIN

The fifty something year old lady walked into the room and heads turned. The men's heads turned towards her and the wive's heads turned to look at their husbands! She was dressed in such a way that her recent breast augmentation was very visible. Though this was a church gathering, she did not seem to feel as if her attire was inappropriate. Instead of being concerned with propriety, she was more interested in enjoying the attention directed her way.

More than any of us realize, our adult behavior develops by our unmet emotional needs. It also forms by those needs that are most important to us. For example, the woman just mentioned no doubt has a deep need for approval or attention. She works very hard to make sure that need will be met.

All of us experience the spiritual and emotional pain I have been talking about. As humans, we do not like pain. Our normal human response is to **"medicate" that pain.** At the first sign of a headache, we take our favorite pain killer. Each of us works regularly on making sure our most pressing needs are met, though few of us realize we are doing that.

My theory is that during our formative years, we begin to find the way to dull the pain of our unmet needs. We also need to numb the pain of our own wrong choices. The bottom line is **you and I enjoy pleasure more than pain**! I am going to show you how this works through my own experience.

Just through living my life and having a variety of experiences, as a little kid I discovered things I found enjoyable. Often simply because of our sinful nature we will be drawn to one thing more than another. That nature shows up in numerous ways.

One time, when I was only about five years old, my dad and I were looking through a trunk that contained some WWII memorabilia. I was sitting real close to Dad and it was a nice father/son moment. Then dad pulled out a pack of postcards from all over the world he had gathered as a soldier. He threw the stack down in front of me and I began to look at the pictures of the places on the postcards. Then part way into the stack, I came upon some that had pictures of ladies who were partially undressed. I remember all the strong feelings I experienced back then, so strong that nearly 50 years later, I still remember very vividly. I loved the feeling of being close to Dad and sharing in some very personal memories he had. I remember really enjoying the shape of the women's bodies. It was an early, very pleasant memory that confused me. It was a special moment with my dad that was sexualized. I don't believe for a minute this was intentional on my dad's part, but it affected me nonetheless.

As I grew older, I remember a junior high school friend who pulled me aside to show me something he had stolen from a hardware store. I looked on in amazement at this magazine he had that contained numerous pictures of women in various stages of undress, and I liked it.

Eventually, in those years, I began to accumulate a couple of those magazines of my own that I hid in my bedroom closet.

I was on the wrestling team in junior high school. Our team practiced in the evening. Sometimes when I came home from practice at night no one would be home. I was afraid during those times. My sense of security was really shaken. I would turn on all the lights, lock the doors and even remember loading a pellet gun and holding it close for protection.

Once I gathered my own stash of magazines in the closet, almost magically, when I was alone and those scary feelings would come over me, **my mind would shift** to the magazines in the closet. Then instead of fear, excitement began to build and I would look at those magazines and **feel pleasure rather than fear**. Over the years then, those images of partially unclothed, smiling women became my place of comfort when I was in emotional pain. I always could find a woman who would smile at me, and show me her assets, as if I were important to her. She never rejected me or belittled me, she never made me feel like I was "less than."

A behavior pattern then begins to form. **Feel pain, run for the pleasure.** When the pleasure creates a pain of its own the next day, it takes more pleasure to decrease that new pain. You can see what a vicious cycle this becomes. Usually, until major work is done, it is very difficult to even recognize this pattern of behavior in us. The truth is, when living in this pattern, **we are not living life on God's terms.** We have not acquired the necessary life skills to handle the disappointments and painful feelings that are common to all human beings on the planet. One really big problem is, you and I can never meet spiritual or emotional needs with physical things. It just doesn't work that way.

When someone says they feel they don't have choice, or they **feel driven** to do something almost against their will, it is simply because they have **trained their subconscious mind** that whenever pain is present, the switch trips in the brain and pleasure is sought out for relief of the emotional pain they are experiencing.

It is my belief that every human being follows this pattern. It could very well be the deep meaning of the Scripture that says, "All we like sheep have gone astray, we have all turned to our own way." (Isaiah 53:6) As we develop, we discover what it is that makes us feel better when we have emotional pain. Once you learn this concept, you can spot what others have chosen as their "drug of choice."

It is difficult to hide that you are an emotional eater or that you escape through drugs or alcohol. Some of the pleasure buttons, like shopping, working or playing a sport, are more socially acceptable. You can see that a man has tried to meet all his feelings of inadequacy by accomplishment and bragging. Often the older a man gets, "the better he was" in his story telling about yester year. You can spot a woman who always got the attention she craved by her physical attributes. This is especially noticeable as she gets older and still tries to use the same approach!

In our culture, there are many things that people use to numb the pain. The most recognized are drugs, alcohol, gambling and other "vices." However, the truth is, anything we do in a compulsive way to medicate some pain, is the exact same dynamic. I have determined that in essence, **we all are drug addicts**. Some ingest drugs, some inject drugs and some of us create our own internal drug rush through this escapist behavior! Science tells us those behaviors cause a chemical mix of adrenaline and endorphins that fire our brains up like a narcotic!

In recovery work there is a slogan: "I've got good news and bad news. The good news is you don't have to run to your drug of choice anymore, the bad news is that isn't really your problem!"

Many times, we think, "If I could just stop looking at porn, over eating, working too much, drinking etc. etc. then life would be great." When you understand the concept I am presenting, you will begin to see that "pleasurable" activity is not your major problem. **The major issue is, learning how to process emotional pain in a healthy way.**

As I finish on this normal human response to pain, I want to address something false. Someone will say, "I just have an addictive personality." That simply is not true. Anyone who says that line is saying, "I have some unresolved hurt in my life that I keep running from!" Here is another truth. You may have a medicine of "first choice." However, if you are hurting, and it is not available, you will find some other source to numb the pain. If the root issues are ignored, if healing does not happen at a deep level, if you do not learn how to face pain, you may stop one unhealthy way of medicating, but you will replace it with another. You simply trade compulsions; you have not really figured it out yet.

Before moving into where this pattern of behavior will lead us, I want to take the next two chapters to look more fully at pain. Chapter Seven will deal with subtle forms of pain and what they mean. Chapter Eight is going to look at the harsh realities of strong pain.

Chapter Seven
SUBTLE KINDS OF PAIN

Lance Dodds, in his book, *The Heart of Addiction,* builds a strong case for what fuels addictive behavior. I remember how that explanation resonated with me. The pain Dodds describes is feelings of **inadequacy**. For a man, being in a position where some action is called for, and not knowing what to do, creates an emotional pain that is so subtle, yet cuts to his core. As John Eldredge writes in *Wild at Heart,* the one question every man asks is, "do I have what it takes?" So, when I am put in a situation where it is my responsibility to do something and I do not know what to do, the answer comes back to me, "Scott, you are not adequate!" The voice in my head tells me I am in too deep. That sense of inadequacy will cause a person to spend hours attempting to escape through their "pleasure of choice." They will rarely tell you what is wrong, that would mean they actually do not measure up.

Imagine now someone who heard from his father or mother growing up, "you'll never amount to anything," being put in a position at work that requires decision making. He or she is unsure what to do. The feelings of uncertainty cause inaction. His or her worst fear is realized; the parent's prophecy is coming true. Many a person at that point will say under their breath, "F_ _ _ this, who needs this job, wife/husband, etc.," and they will be found medicating their pain soon after. I always liked the phrase, "Everything rises and falls on leadership," until I was the leader and it was not rising!

Another form of a more subtle pain is **boredom**. Mastering the first six chapters of this book, you will begin to identify your own patterns of behavior and the times you are most likely to run to your medicine. On the surface, boredom is just boredom. I'm not busy enough. "An idle mind is the devil's workshop," Grandma used to say. At the core of boredom is a much deeper pain. It is **purposelessness**. That is one reason why Rick Warren's book, *The Purpose Driven Life*, has been such a huge success. People were created to have purpose. Boredom is merely a symptom that our lives are not being fueled by a passionate purpose. If it were, our minds would be whirring with ideas and thoughts of how to accomplish that purpose, rather than wondering what to do next. However, during times of what we call boredom, we are uncomfortable. and we tend to occupy ourselves with that which we find most desirable, most pleasurable.

Often while running to pleasure from one of these subtle

pains, we create our own **secondary levels of pain. Guilt, shame, and beating yourself up** for doing something you vowed not to do again. The conversation runs on autopilot in your head. "How could you do that again? What if someone finds out what I am really like? I told you, you were a loser!" Therefore, like a dog returning to his vomit, to quiet those voices, we find ourselves running right back to the temporary pleasure that fixes everything...for the moment at least.

So, I am the lead pastor of a congregation. I was trained for ministry in a school that said, "Some of you will pastor a church of two hundred people one day." My first church in its best days had about seventy people. When I assumed the leadership of my second church it was two hundred regular attendees, but was declining. It had more committees than my first church had members. Now, fast-forward five years. I find myself as the leader of an organization of 450-550 people and growing. There are so many organizational needs, facility needs and people's personal needs, that I feel very inadequate and somewhat overwhelmed. We had overhauled the entire church, which created many angry people who wanted my head on a platter. I did feel competent at preaching my message, so that is what I did. Our team did a great job planning message series' and I worked hard at doing my sermon. Nevertheless, when I got it done, though there was a ton to do, **I did not have a plan of action; I did not know where to begin anymore.** Often I would feel bored or inadequate or both. By now I had found some creative ways to look at some enticing pictures without letting myself believe I was really looking for them! Denial is a strong thing.

I prepared my own PowerPoint slide shows to go with sermons. I would search the Internet looking for images to insert on my slides and often, my searches would bring up images that were less than wholesome. I spent enough hours looking for slideshow pictures but always hoping to see some picture of a woman that would give me an adrenaline charge. With the time wasted, I could have organized and charted a path for a much larger organization, if only I had admitted my need for some help and sought it out.

Though I will deal with this fully in Chapter Eleven, all I had to do was humble myself to find the help I needed to get our church to the next level. My pride kept me wanting to be, "the man," without the need to seek much in the way of outside help. Amazingly, after facing humiliation, I was open and willing to get the help I needed to move the church forward.

Finally, I want to consider the situation of "treating myself" to my pleasure pill, which began to seem common. I am starting to wonder if I needed much excuse at all, but really, when you begin to untangle the web, you discover there is always a reason for our behavior.

What is it about eating a huge Thanksgiving Dinner that makes it not complete without dessert? In the same way, a very common time for me to run to my pleasure source was to **celebrate** something that I did well. Joe Dallas, in his book, *The Game Plan*, spends considerable time unfolding this concept of **entitlement**.

It is the feeling that I deserve some reward for working hard or doing a good job. It is just one more subtle thing that can lead us to run to "our cracked well" that really does not have what we need. By now each reader should understand this slogan, "You can never get enough of what you don't need."

I want to take a little time in the next chapter to look at pain that is not subtle. It is so strong it shouts at you to relieve it some way, any way.

Chapter Eight
STRONG PAIN—
STRONG MEDICINE

For some reading this book, everything I have written about seems so easy. You may be thinking if my only problems were a few unmet emotional needs, I'd have it made. I know a man who had begun attending church. He had not yet been able to accept Christ into his life because when we talked about God being our father, it repulsed him. This man was a survivor. He was in his forties but still carried deep wounds from the consistent beatings he received as a boy by his drunken father. He talked to me in the halls of a hospital one day and said, "I just can't forgive my father for what he did, and I will never forgive him."

On another occasion, a young couple had begun attending our church. They often loitered after services and then would leave. One day, they finally ask if they could talk with me. They began to tell me the horror story of this young wife, who was sexually abused at the hands of her own father from the age of four until she reached puberty. Her sister had the same experience. Now there were two granddaughters living in that home and she was afraid the same thing might be happening. I assured her unless her father had gotten major help, I could guarantee it was happening. She told me of a relative that stood by and allowed this to go on with her and her sister. I challenged her not to repeat the same mistake. This young lady and her sister finally got the courage and went to the police. Their father is now in prison due to their courage. But, can you imagine the depth of pain and damage that was inflicted on these girls growing up with all the fear, abuse and shame they must have felt?

Many people who experience such traumatic events in their lives will be driven in ways that should be obvious to anyone who has eyes to see. For example, the young lady was meticulous about the way she looked and kept her home. **That desire for perfection is often an attempt to control your world.** This type of control is most appealing to someone who has previously had no control of anything and is **afraid he or she might lose control again.**

The man beaten by his father was driven to excel. You could not talk to him for more than a short time and he would tell you of his athletic accomplishments. **He felt so beat down, he was trying to convince others, and himself, that he was adequate.**

I feel fortunate to have never faced any of those deep

traumatic events myself. In some ways, I do not blame anyone who has gone through something like this for doing the best they can to survive.

The question is, can someone who has been traumatized like this ever do more than survive? Is it possible for those people to thrive?

For those with strong pain, the level of pain and the levels of the medicine required are much greater than the average. However, **the mechanics of how all this works is the same no matter the kind of pain or even the medicine of choice.** The road to healing is the same. It may be a bit longer for some than others. It may require a more experienced adventure guide for some than others. Just as the pattern of pain and medicating are the same, the road to healing is also the same.

So you are not left wondering, both the people mentioned above, the young lady sexually abused by her father and the gentleman beaten by his dad, came to a place of facing their pain and growing to a healthier way of living.

Most readers at this point are saying, "What is the solution?" The solution comes through understanding the process and the things that will be taught in the remaining chapters.

I want you to know there is no "silver bullet." We will look at that concept closely in Chapter Ten. First, I want to show you what I believe to be one of the greatest damaging effects of following the natural human method of dealing with pain. That is coming up next.

Chapter Nine

MASTERING COMPARTMENTALIZATION; LIVING WITH SECRETS

We sat in the cozy loft, about eight couples in a life group. A life group is a group of people who meet to do a Bible Study and share life together. I ask the ladies in the group if they felt they knew their husbands entirely. Every one of the ladies said, they intuitively knew there was a part of their husband they did not know. I asked if they could put a percentage on it. Each of them said there is probably fifteen to twenty percent that she believed he kept secret from her. Each lady said it shook her security, wondering what that void was, but he would not reveal it. Most men are not relational enough or intuitive enough to understand how their wives could know the men are keeping secrets. Women have a sixth sense that is extremely accurate. Most women would say it would be much easier to deal with whatever the secret is than to live with the uncertainty of not knowing. It is one of the greatest ways to damage a relationship, I know, living with a secret compartment.

Men are not the only ones who attempt to hide how they "medicate" their pain. I have counseled some ladies in the past that told me their secrets. One in particular I remember went shopping to deaden her pain. She attempted to escape the emotional pain through the rush she experienced purchasing something new. She was elaborate in her attempts to move money around from credit card to credit card to keep her spending habits secret.

Generally, if you and I have a medicine of choice, we guard it with all we are worth. Denial is often not so much that we do not realize what we are doing, but to admit it is out of control would require we do something about it. Therefore, we hide it. The more we think it is not acceptable, the more care we take to guard the secret.

Some things are easier to keep secret than others are. I used to say I was glad my "medicine of choice" was not alcohol; at least I could look at pornography and drive under control! However, probably more than one man has had a wreck straining his neck to get a better look at some girl.

So, our medication practices remain **a secret compartment** of our lives, while we are fully functioning in all the other necessary areas, at least for a while. **All people who medicate**

and guard secrets are also deceivers by necessity. The guy sitting up late at night looking at Internet porn has to make up a little "white lie" to tell his wife what time he came to bed and what he was doing up so late. Later, if she finds some damning link on the computer, he has to blame it on something or someone else. The person who eats for comfort does not reveal how often they stop at the fast food place for a snack. We all really hammered President Clinton for lying on national TV when he said, "I did not have sex with that woman, Monica Lewinsky," but it was probably **more from seeing our own reflection** than his wrongdoing!

Many scandals have rocked the church world. Remember the big ones? Jimmy Bakker and Jimmy Swaggart and now the latest, Ted Haggard. Many less prominent ministers failed morally, bringing their sin and humiliation into the public arena.

So how does that happen?

Just like this!

All pastors are simply people who have developed in the same way you did. We have unmet needs which creates pain. We make sinful choices and have the pain of them. We have life pain that is experienced. We begin a pattern of medicating our pain with whatever pleasure pill does the trick for us.

Then we open our lives to the gospel of Jesus Christ, often hoping He will instantly remove our vice. **He usually does not!** Now we are Christians and our behavior is not acceptable among Christians. In many ways, becoming a Christian makes this battle worse. The message preached is everything is new, the old goes away. So, what do we do when we find the battle is raging and we have failed? We learn to hide it better! Then we develop the fine art of compartmentalization.

Often we have gifts that propel us to be in the public eye. We can speak and have a hunger to learn, often to figure ourselves out! **Our gifts exceed our character.** We become Christians who learn to serve. Some are promoted all the way to the stage and leading the organization, **WHILE STILL MEDICATING OUR PAIN THE SAME WAY WE ALWAYS HAVE!** We become leaders in an organization filled with people who criticize, belittle and gossip about us. We beat ourselves up for our weakness and failure, we cry out to God for deliverance. We promise never to do it again. We do it again! We hide it! We preach on Sunday! We isolate ourselves. We believe that if people really knew who we were, we would be toast, so we perfect our public image and guard our private self. Too many times the additional pain and fears that come from living that way, just fuel the pattern.

I know this pattern is prevalent in many pastor's lives in our country. What fills our pulpits also fills our pews! One of the reasons many in church never really get involved is this, they come to church to keep up their public image, but down deep, they know **Christianity has not worked for them,** so why go to any great length to invite others, or to give sacrificially or to go overboard giving time to volunteer?

Finally, this compartmentalization does one more thing to us in a negative way. I believe having intimacy with God and with any other significant person in life, especially my spouse, requires a deep heart connection. All anyone can really know of someone else comes from observation and revelation. In other words, my wife can observe how I am and I can reveal my heart to her, the two are not necessarily the same. **The more honest I share who I am, the greater the intimacy.** The more I compartmentalize, the less genuine intimacy.

This secret place is protected and kept secret often for much of a person's adult life. The secret place allows access by no one else. The public image is in contrast moral, bright and filled with all kinds of surface charm. Then God's patience wears thin and He allows the secret closet to be flushed out to the public eye. Everyone is very shocked. The spouse may feel like they are married to a stranger. Often the spouse will say, "I never really knew him or her." To some degree that is true. You knew the carefully managed image, but not the secret place.

As long as compartmentalization is happening, there really **cannot be true intimacy** with God or with any other human being. It just is not possible. True intimacy is what we all are seeking. True intimacy is that safe relational place to be known and loved for just being you. This compartmentalization skill, highly developed, will allow a person to function for sometime with one foot in both worlds.

According to Scripture, not everyone will be found out in this life, but all will be revealed in the next (1 Timothy 5:24). Often, because God has greater plans for us than we know, our gracious

Father will allow the cover to be blown and our secret compartment exposed.

Usually, when that happens, **we become willing** to do what it takes to make things right. Unfortunately, for some, the increased pain of exposure just creates a greater need to medicate and the cycle goes on.

Let's turn the corner now and begin looking at how this pattern can change. How can we live life on God's terms? The first awareness must be there is no quick fix.

Chapter Ten
NO SILVER BULLETS

We are a nation obsessed with the idea we can fix things quickly and painlessly. One person would say, "I'm one hundred pounds overweight and I'm looking for a pill that allows me to eat all I want, do no exercise and lose three pounds a night while I sleep!" Another may say, "It has taken me five years to get in debt up to my eyeballs, but I want to get out of it by the end of next week!" Then yet another, "I've been damaging my marriage for years by totally disregarding my spouse's feelings, but now I'm ready to make it right so give me the "silver bullet" pastor, and honey, fall in line!"

One of the appeals to the more flamboyant side of Christianity, is the idea that one trip to the altar, one whack on the head, one supernatural experience and all my issues will be fixed.

Many people are spending too much money playing state lotteries thinking if I can just hit the big one my problems will be solved. You all know the statistics on that! My theory is if you are struggling to manage, the little you have, how is getting more money going to help you? You will just have more to mismanage.

There is a group of people very common in evangelical churches. People who have stopped one or more destructive outside behavior by sheer force of will because they know it is the right thing to do. In recovery, this approach is called, "white knuckling." The idea is you are still as sick as ever, you just probably changed medications (remember the good news/bad news?). I remember a guy who was an alcoholic, abusive, clearly had some deep issues that needed work. He quit drinking alcohol, switching to O'Doul's, a non-alcohol version of beer. His relationships were still terrible yet he was quick to tell anyone how they needed Jesus in their lives, so they could have what he had. I often wondered exactly what it was he had, and knew I certainly did not want any of whatever it was. I was quite sure it was not Jesus!

So, I have myself in a mess. I've invested a lot of emotion in another woman. I have neglected my own wife, and I'm in a deeper funk than I know. I decide what I need is to see a counselor. I schedule the first appointment in my life with a professional counselor. I ask him two big questions. First, are you a Christian? Second, do you live on this side of town? He answers "Yes" to the first question and "No" to the second, so we have a deal. I told him the truth of what was going on and that no one else knew. I told him all the lines I'd crossed with a woman who was not my wife. I told him I was the pastor of a growing church.

Even though, down deep I knew enough to know there was no quick, clean and painless way out, I still had hopes he had a "silver bullet" for me. Give me two steps and a prayer and lets get this session over. **Make it as painless as possible Dr.!** Do you have a pill that will fix me? I am writing over six years after that initial meeting with the counselor, and life is much different now. However, the journey towards spiritual and emotional health has been a long slow one.

Could I inject some hope for you? The Lord has forgiven me of my sin; Gayle has forgiven me for my sin. Just recently, I have actually released myself from my past sin and have made a choice to look forward. As our pastor said, "I threw an interception but the game isn't over." I added, "I believe I may have a "Hail Mary" left in me!"

I do have a regret. I wish I would have been able to **embrace the window of time** God gave me, from becoming a Christian until my train wreck, to see **He was giving me space to humble myself** before Him and do whatever it took to get healthy. Instead, my story would read more like Proverbs 5. The downward spiral, the crash and burn, the humiliation and heartache that came because of not dealing with my sin have been huge.

My personal mission now is to help all the people I can, learn about how all this works, so they can connect the dots in their own lives, and be spared the crash and burn. **You do not have to hit rock bottom to change!** I am going to look at the options available to you in the next chapter.

Chapter Eleven
HUMBLE YOURSELF
OR FACE HUMILIATION

When I am motivated by fear, my behavior guarantees the results I feared are one hundred percent sure to happen. I did not humble myself and tell my struggle to others because I feared what they would think. I feared I would lose my career. So, I did not humble myself, I rather lived in a way that I have just written ten chapters about. I faced humiliation because I did not humble myself. Fall on the rock or the rock will fall on you!

Most people will extend grace to a person who humbles himself or herself and admits they have been wrong. Few people have much sympathy for someone who plays the game all the way to the explosion when the cover is blown off, the scandal breaks and you're caught. Then you not only have been found out doing wrong stuff, you are a liar too. Now your repentance is suspect.

Did he repent because he got caught and had no option? Is he still just playing? There is something far nobler in the eyes of people, when a person breaks and comes clean. Another slogan in recovery says "humility before humiliation."

The God of the universe gives us that option as well. "Humble yourselves before the Lord and He will lift you up." (James 4:10) Why then is it such a rarity to ever find someone, even in Scripture who humbles themselves first? Adam sinned and hid in the bushes and blamed Eve. He did everything but humble himself. David did not admit to anything until Nathan, the prophet, stuck his finger in David's face and called him on his sin. Job did not acknowledge his arrogant attitude until God showed up and called him on the carpet for about two chapters of overwhelming questions. On and on the story goes, few people confess much of anything without being caught.

I did the same thing. I told no more than I had to until I was crushed by the love of God. (I'll tell you that story in Chapter Fourteen).

When I think of how God responds to the person who humbles himself before Him, I think of the prodigal son story as recorded in Luke 15. The prodigal experienced humiliation as he fed the hogs and desired to eat their food. His friends all left him when the money ran out; he found himself left to wallow in the slop of a hog pen. The enemy whispers in our ear, never admit to anything, but then we are humiliated when our sin becomes known. When the prodigal decided that he had sinned and wanted to ask his father for forgiveness there is a beautiful picture of how God treats those who humble themselves and turn from their sin. The story says, the father saw the son coming when he was yet a long way off.

The father ran to him and embraced him. Listen to this: the father sent a servant home to get his finest robe, his shoes and a ring for his son. While far from home and away from the older brother's gaze, the father cleaned up the son and dressed him in his finest. No one would ever see the son in his humiliated state, only the father. When he brings the son home, no one else knows how low the son went. Only the father knows how low the boy went, but he is not talking about it anymore, he is too busy celebrating the change of heart and the boy's return!

It is a wise thing to humble yourself and seek out some direction for dealing with the pain in your life. It is always safe to bring your hurt before the Father and ask Him for wisdom in overcoming the patterns of medicating you have learned. He wants to set you free. It is always a very bright thing to humble yourself before the Lord. He will lift you up. Just as the father in the prodigal son story had a much better life to offer the son than the son found wandering on his own, our Father has so much with which He wants to bless our lives.

One of the benefits of humbling yourself is you get to choose who learns about your struggles. You can go to a trusted person and reveal the depth of your hurt and despair. When you hold on and wait until you are humiliated, you lose the privilege of how wide the circle is that finds out about you. As my friend Willie says, "only two parties will know about you, Democrats and Republicans!"

I invite you, whoever and wherever you are right now, put this book down, confess your failure to the Lord, and within the next twenty-four hours confess your failure to another trusted human being. It will be the beginning of your healing. James 5:16 says, "Confess your faults to one another and you will be healed!" There is something powerful about bringing those secrets into the light. **You are only as sick as your secrets**. When you have no secrets, you will find that you become much healthier emotionally and spiritually.

Once we become willing to humble ourselves, the first step toward a new life has begun. In the next chapter, I am going to teach you about one of the greatest concepts toward freedom in Scripture.

Chapter Twelve
WHAT SURRENDER LOOKS LIKE
AND HOW TO DO IT

I bowed my knee and accepted Christ into my life as a twenty-one year old. To the best of my ability, I trusted Him for my eternal salvation and deliverance from sin. Over the early years, and even into my time in Bible College, I regularly asked Christian leaders why I felt like I was holding something back. One night in a mission's conference, I asked the speaker about my spiritual struggle. I told him that I felt that I was not giving the Lord one hundred percent; rather I always felt that I was holding out some part of me. The missionary told me to "join the club."

I believe the Lord uses everything in life to teach us, especially once He has our attention. During my stay at the counseling center in Florida, the Lord taught me what surrender looks like. I never fully understood what surrender was or how to do it. The

Lord showed me that I had given myself more fully to a another flawed human, than I had ever given myself to Him, the Creator of the universe! The message I heard was, "as much as you have given yourself emotionally to this woman, I want that much given to me." It was as if God used my devotion to my sin to teach me about devotion to Him! Once I understood what surrender was, it became easy to transfer that loyalty to Him and then to Gayle and finally to my commitment to ministry.

Before, I protected my true self. I was always afraid to reveal my whole self to anyone for fear of rejection. God used a another person to teach me about surrender! Isn't it a teaching principle to take someone from the known to the unknown? That is what the Father did with me. From that point on, I knew what He wanted and what surrender meant. He was safe and I could trust Him with my full being.

Think about how you have trusted your self to your medicine of choice. You have guarded and given yourself to your pain relief in a way you have not trusted yourself to anyone or anything else. You always feel safe and comforted when in the grasp of your "drug of choice." In reality, all of our methods of medicating then become **idolatry** to us. They step into a role that only God really has the right or ability to fill. **Take the surrender you have known to your medication and transfer that same commitment to God.**

Once the lights go on in your head, it becomes obvious you've trusted a piece of paper with a picture on it to comfort your pain more than the living, loving God who created you.

You have believed a shopping spree could do something deep inside for you instead of believing the Savior who willingly died in your place could do more.

You actually believed a piece of chocolate cake could fill the lonely places in your life more than a living Lord could ever fill you.

Go from your known to your unknown. The way you get giddy when you know you are going to indulge yourself in whatever your medication has been, surrender that same level of belief and trust to the living Lord.

The reason we often run to non-living things for relief is that we are afraid any living, thinking being would judge us, reject us, shame us and never understand what we are facing. Generally, we have the evidence to back up that belief by our experience with other people.

What if in the grand scheme of things, God allows this normal pattern of human behavior to happen to show us how empty it really is? What if the whole stage is set with a logical outcome in mind? That outcome being as Jeremiah 2:13 says, we discover all the wells we thought had living water were cracked. They do not produce the expected outcome. Insanity is doing the same thing and expecting a different outcome. So, let me ask you Dr. Phil's question. **"How is that working for you?"** Are you happy, joyous and free when you medicate your pain? Has your pattern made you feel healthy and whole? Has it really made all your relationships function much better? Has it built up your confidence and made you feel like you are really a competent person?

There is no "silver bullet," but the next chapter is the closet thing you will find to a formula for overcoming this pattern of broken living. The key that opens the door to great new levels of growth will be next.

As we get ready to head into major life transformation, would you in your mind and heart become willing to give God a chance to do for you what you have trusted your "medicine" to do? Would you at least transfer the same level of confidence to Him that up until now you have demonstrated in your escape?

"Lord, I'm a little afraid. I've tried so many times to stop this merry-go-round and get off, but it has never happened. I will at least surrender to You, as fully as I have to _____ up until now. I'm going to trust You can help me begin to live in a healthier way for you, me and everyone in my sphere of influence."

Chapter Thirteen
FACE YOUR PAIN;
RUN TO YOUR FATHER

If you have been in a car wreck and taken to an emergency room, the normal practice is **not** to give you anything for pain. **It is easier to diagnose what the injuries inside you are by your pain!**

In treating drug and alcohol addiction, the first step to recovery is "detox." Detox is putting you somewhere for several days to a couple weeks to get the drugs and alcohol totally out of your system. The reason for that is, as long as the drug is in your system you are numb to what the real issues are in your life. You are not capable of dealing with the pain that is driving you to drug or drink, as long as you are medicated.

It is no different for any of us. As long as we do whatever we do to kill our pain, we never fully feel it, or face it and grow through it. **Every time we run to a painkiller, we pass up an opportunity to grow** through a life stretching experience. Every time I run to escape by dulling the feeling of inadequacy, I give up running to the Father and others to learn how to become more adequate!

The major key to your future is this choice. **I will not medicate my pain anymore. Instead, I will face the pain. I will run to the Father.** I will run to a close friend. I will run to someone who can teach me what I am lacking.

Joseph's story, found in Genesis 37-50, shows us we do not have to crash and burn to surrender our pain and let God shape us and accomplish His purposes through us. Joseph was sold into slavery by his brothers. He clung to his faith and God blessed him even as a slave. He was wrongly accused by his master's wife and thrown in prison. He did not medicate. He faced the pain and ran to his Father. The Father blessed him and elevated him from prisoner to Prime Minister of Egypt! Joseph is a picture of what happens when we allow pain to shape us and teach us rather than medicating it. God uses the pain in our lives as an impetus to growth.

A more common story would be one like David's story or Peter's story. **Both men protected their image to a breaking point.** Following the humiliation, they both chose to be shaped by the pain, humbled, broken but now more useful to the Father than before. Unfortunately, not everyone who goes through a crushing experience chooses to embrace the pain as a mentor. Judas, the betrayer of Christ, also had an opportunity to be humiliated and exposed, but instead of embracing pain and becoming a humble servant, he took his life in the ultimate escape.

My story goes like this: From the treatment center, I emailed my wife a note saying, "The Lord has shown me He won't let me run from the mess I made. He will not let me stay either. I need to build the church to not need me and He will let me know when it is time to go." Three years after the failure, having confessed fully to a couple counselors, my wife, and a few close friends, I had received a *Defining Moments* CD from The Willow Creek Association. The CD's focus was moral failure among pastors. When I heard it, I felt like someone punched me in the stomach. I knew it was time. I asked each of my staff pastors to listen to that CD and then we would talk. We decided it was time to reveal the full story to our elders. After three weeks of meetings and phone calls attempting to figure out what to do with me, the elders and I agreed it was time to resign the church I had served for twelve years. Gayle and I moved from Virginia to Florida and I went to work in a large building supply center. I was going to head into a time of grieving, loss, depression and pain like I had never known.

I determined **I was going to face the pain with no medication and allow God to shape** me through it. I would face the ugly truth about myself. I would allow Him to show me whatever He felt I needed to learn. I invited Him to do in me what needed to be done.

When you make a decision to face the pain and run to the Father instead of medicating, the Lord takes you to a new place in your development. **It was exhilarating to sense the Father's pleasure and presence even in the midst of the soul wrenching pain.**

Joe Dallas, in his book, *The Game Plan,* gives a simple doable daily way to focus on your new way of living. Instead of focusing on what you are saying "No" to, figure out what your big, "Yes," will be.

For me, every morning I pray. *"Lord, today I want to have intimacy and freedom before you. I don't want to have to hide in the bushes. I want to be able to hear your voice and enjoy you. I also want to know the freedom with my wife, Gayle, that comes when I have no secrets. I know the things I run to naturally, steal the things I really want. So, just for today, this twenty-four hour period, help me say, "Yes" to You and Gayle and "No" to..."* I have my own list of items that I commit to twenty-four hours of saying no. You will need to develop your own.

In the next chapter, I need to tell you a story that set the stage for me to feel I could trust Him enough with this process.

Do not miss the point of this chapter. It is key to everything. Here it is one more time:

FACE YOUR PAIN WITH NO MEDICATION. RUN TO YOUR FATHER AND LET HIM SHAPE YOU THROUGH THE PAIN!

Chapter Fourteen
HEALING DEEP WOUNDS

Remember my story of looking through the fence as my dad left to go fishing? Throughout my young life, I felt the message I was not good enough. That message came to me from many sources. I was always very small for my age and I think that contributed as well. I had a deep insecurity that often came out as pride. I compensated by trying to act tough, lifting weights to look strong, excelling at sports, and posturing as if I was more than I was. That feeling of not being adequate followed me everywhere. I graduated first in my class from Bible College, but down deep still did not feel like I was competent to lead. **I excelled more from the fear of failure than because of proficiency.** I regularly told some of the people on my staff at the church, "I feel like the wheels could fall off this organization at anytime." I lived under that cloud.

It was a heck of a thing to be the lead person in an organization that had multi-faceted issues and feeling as if I was not qualified or capable of creating solutions. I generally felt the same way as a husband and as a father. I knew it was up to me to be what my wife and family needed, but down deep, I often felt I did not have what they needed. I honestly believe John Eldredge hit this one for many guys, in *Wild at Heart*. Eldredge calls this the "father wound." Eldredge believes for a young man to believe he is adequate, only the significant males in his life can pass that down to him. I believe there is some validity to his concept. I personally don't believe for most guys it is a lack of skills as much as a lack of belief in ourselves.

So, I have been given this huge responsibility and opportunity by God to lead this awesome church. The church has grown over many years in a growing community. People are coming, but many people also leave. I hear the criticisms of those leaving much louder than I hear the praises of those coming. I medicate my pain. I medicate my feelings of inadequacy. Now, a chink in my armor has been exposed. I am partially found out. I am dead inside. God feels a million miles away. I am on a beach jogging in the early morning. I have already been in counseling three hours a day for four days. I feel nothing but numbness. The first day at the center, I rode a bicycle seventy-five miles in a feverish effort to run from myself but to no avail. **The problem was that anywhere I went, there I was!**

I had not given much thought to anything but my own desperation. I had two weeks at this place and if nothing changed, I had already decided I would disappear into South Florida and no one would know what ever happened to me. A singer named Jimmy Buffet sang about a place in Florida named, "Margaritaville," and I would attempt to find it!

I have never heard an audible voice from God. However, this early morning on the beach as I jogged, a very clear voice impression came through my mind that I know was the voice of God. His message to me, though six years ago now, still brings tears to my eyes and shivers up my spine.

"I love you, son!"

I was cut to the core of my being. Like Peter when the rooster crowed, I wept bitterly for probably thirty minutes. I could not gather myself or stop the flood of brokenness. It was as if a skilled surgeon had just opened the deepest wound at the core of who I was. My tears flushed that open wound and cleaned it out. I still am in shock at those first words. I would expect to hear, "after all I've done for you, how could you?" But never, "I love you, son."

At this point of my life, I had been a Christian for twenty-five years. I had studied the Bible formally for seven years. I had preached to many that God loved them. I had sung, "Jesus loves me this I know, for the Bible tells me so." However, I never had experienced that truth. I never really felt at the core of my being that all-encompassing love, until that moment. At the lowest point of my human existence, when in my mind I was the least lovable, when I would expect to hear any other message that berated me, **He chose to reveal His love to me!**

I did not deserve to hear that message, but it was a revealing of the heart of God. He is love (1 John 4:8). He showed that love openly "while we were yet in our sins, He sent His Son to die in our place" (Romans 5:8).

I believe this experience of the clear biblical truth of **God's love for me has become the foundation** to give me the ability to trust Him while working through my past pain, and any current situation that comes, without medicating.

The opening, cleansing and healing of that deep wound has changed me in some major ways. It has given me the courage and trust to invite God to continue showing me things that I need to see. I have come to believe He is a very safe person, who will be gentle in the process of helping me to become more like Him. He has made this adventure of living life on God's terms and in His ways, really feel doable.

Every little girl and every little boy has a longing to know Daddy loves them. That he is their hero and protector. That he is proud of them. Maybe many of you never really felt that kind of security and love growing up.

Can you hear the voice of The Father right now speaking into your life? **"I love you, son." "I love you, honey."**

I recently heard an interview with Charles Stanley, author and pastor. He said he was fifty-two years old the first time he personally experienced God's love!

I would encourage you right now, by faith to believe that God is love and that He loves you more than you could know. I would also encourage you to ask Him to allow you the joy of experiencing that love at the core of who you are.

After this experience, I discovered a passage in the Bible that has become fascinating to me. It is located in John 15: 9-11. Jesus said, "I have loved you even as the Father has loved me. Remain in my love. When you obey me, you remain in my love, just as I obey my Father and remain in his love. I have told you this so that you will be filled with my joy. Yes, your joy will overflow!

Once you and I have experienced this awesome love, the desire will be to remain in the experience of that love. **Staying inside the boundaries is what allows us to stay in the experience of His love and the result is overflowing joy!**

He began to teach me the reason why there are some boundaries in life. We are not capable of experiencing his deep love and joy when our lives are filled with guilt and shame. Life inside the boundaries frees us to be able to experience how great His love is for us. His love does not change for us when we jump the fence, we just do not get the joy of experiencing His love.

My whole motive for obeying shifted from being afraid of His punishment, to not wanting to ever lose this awesome feeling of being loved and the joy that comes as a result. No, **obedience does not earn his love; it just lets me feel what is already there for me.**

With the deep wound healed and the solid foundation of His love to work from, I am ready to give Him the total freedom to teach me whatever I need to see.

Everything is changing now. I am secure in His love for me. When life throws some pain my way, I face it and run to the Father, rather than medicating. Before, I was not willing to admit the areas I needed to change; now I am inviting Him to keep bringing the life lessons. I have been shocked to see how much work I need to do on myself!

Once we have stopped running to lesser things, the bad news begins. Remember the good news bad news I wrote about earlier? Once the anesthetic is out of our systems, all kinds of pain begin to surface. Dealing with that will be our next chapter.

Chapter Fifteen
THREE-WAY FORGIVENESS

Some of the intense battle has subsided. You have not medicated any pain for a couple months. You notice you are somewhat depressed and there are many thoughts that come rushing into your mind. For some of you, major hurts and wrongs begin to surface. Some will begin to think about people in your life who have done things to you that are very painful. Now it is time to begin dealing with some of the pain that has been fueling your drive to escape all along.

Ever since Adam and Eve ate the fruit, the human family has wanted someone else to blame for our situation. Adam blamed Eve, Eve blamed the snake and we have played the blame game ever since. For this process to help you find peace, blaming must stop and accepting full responsibility needs to begin. You and I have to play the hand we were dealt. We really have no other option. We are one hundred percent responsible for living God's way with the life we have.

Take some time and turn your focus from those who have hurt you, to others you have hurt. I would invite you to put on some quiet background music, get a legal size tablet, and ask God to bring to your mind people you have wronged. Then get quiet and wait. The Lord will begin to float memories to your mind and as He does, write them on your pad.

When I did this exercise, I had more than a full legal sheet filled! When the immensity of your own wrongdoing begins to settle in, I am pleased to tell you, the Father is eager to forgive you for all you have done! Simply realize, Romans 5:6-8 is true, and it is true for you. Jesus Christ died for everything on your list. If you stop denying and start agreeing with God concerning your sin, He will forgive you. A sub point of receiving forgiveness from God is asking those you have hurt to forgive you as well. I call this practice "surrender to win." It generally takes most the fight out of someone, when you beat him or her to the punch by apologizing for the hurt you caused him or her!

Here is how this works. Forget about what they have done to you at this point. That is not your concern. Clear through all that fog and focus on what you did that was hurtful. You simply apologize for what you did. When you do that, often the guard will drop and the other person will begin to apologize for their part. It is something to behold. Rather than escalating a situation, it deflates it.

One time I had a staff person having a rift with a couple in the church. It was escalating, "he said, she said," kind of bickering. I called the staff person into the office and said, "Think through your side of this and find one thing you did wrong." He came up with something like a poor attitude. I said now call the couple up and humble yourself by apologizing for your attitude. He said, "Yeah, but what about what they have done?" I said, "Trust me on this and forget about that a minute. Just do what I ask and watch what happens." He sat in front of me, called, and said, "I've been thinking through our disagreement and I feel I owe you an apology. My attitude has been wrong toward you and I need to ask you to forgive me." I could tell by his expression and the ongoing conversation that it was going well. He told me after the call that they began to apologize for all the stuff they had done! That is what surrender to win looks like.

Once you have received forgiveness from God and others, you are ready to move to the second part of forgiveness. It is impossible to find peace inside when you are allowing someone to live rent free in your head because you cannot or will not forgive them. Often this is extremely difficult for someone who has been severely violated. The inability to release that person causes you to stay in a state of internal angst. I'm going to tell you the story how the guy I referred to earlier who was beaten by his father came to a place of forgiving his dad.

When he met me in the hallway of the hospital and told me of the hatred and inability to forgive his dad that he carried with him, I wondered if I had anything to offer him. He told me of his dad beating him repeatedly. He told me of the fear he felt and nights he actually fled from the house and slept in a field to avoid the beating from his drunken father.

I asked him if he ever saw the old TV show *Andy of Mayberry*. He had seen the show. I said, do you remember Barney Fife? The only prisoner he ever had was Otis, the town drunk. Then one day Barney caught a real criminal robbing the town bank and put him in his jail cell. At first, Barney would be bragging about his exploits, but soon he would realize that having someone in his prison meant that Barney had become a prisoner as well. He had to guard, feed and stay with the prisoner. Barney was a prisoner in his own prison. Finally, a federal Marshall came to Mayberry with a paddy wagon and asked Barney to release the prisoner to him so he could transfer the prisoner to the "big house." With relief, Barney turned over custody to a higher authority. Barney, through releasing the prisoner, became free again himself.

I told him, "God isn't asking you to forgive your dad and release him as if nothing ever happened. He is asking you to release him to the Judge of all the earth who will do right!" I said, "Will you turn the prisoner over to God. He will handle your dad appropriately and you won't have to guard him anymore. Do not set him free; release him to a Higher Authority." He came to me some time later and said, "That silly story gave me the ability to forgive my dad. I have released him!"

By not forgiving those who wrong us, **our peace is replaced by pain**. What we are attempting to do with this writing is turn that around. **Through facing pain, you will find peace.**

The problem with forgiving others and receiving forgiveness from God and those we have wronged, is that it clears everything out of the way except to blame ourselves. The final part of forgiveness is releasing yourself. If you have a tender heart at all and you have done some very hurtful things, the tendency is to beat yourself up. I alluded in the introduction to a message my pastor gave recently. He used the analogy of a football game. It is as if you or I threw an interception at a critical moment of the game. It hurts. We can lie down and quit at that point, or we can look at the game clock and remember the game is not over yet. Yeah, I messed up, but I still have time left to go out and make a difference in the outcome of the game. If God is ultimately the person I have sinned against and He released me, who am I to appeal that decision. It would be like asking a county court to review a Supreme Court Decision! Stop beating yourself up, rather, learn to use every failure as an opportunity to grow. This process will continue throughout our entire earthly life.

I want to examine how that continued progress works in the next chapter.

Chapter Sixteen
PEELING THE ONION

There is a very clear objective God has for everyone who embraces Jesus Christ as his or her Savior. In fact, the Bible actually uses some really strong language in saying that it is already predetermined for every Christian that one day **we will become like Jesus Christ** (Romans 8:29). Philippians 1:6, actually promises that **God will complete the task** He started in us. First John three reveals when the task will be completed, "**When we see Him**, we will be like Him." **From now until eternity, God will be working to reshape us into His own image.** We will look at that further in Chapter Seventeen.

Here is the deal. It does not take a genius to see that if the goal is to be like Jesus in all our thoughts, actions and relationships, **none of us is there yet!** No one you have ever known or seen, no pastor, no holy person has arrived! Unless someone is the exact, spitting image of Jesus, there is work to be done!

Why then do most church people pretend they have it together? For the same reason you and I do! Our churches have not been safe to live life the way it really is. Church has not really been a bunch of people together admitting there is so much work to do in our lives. Church has not been a place where a person beaten and broken by life can come in, without being judged. Church has the reputation for being a place that shoots its own wounded!

When I was first introduced to Recovery, and went and sat in some rooms with people who started their talk by saying, "Hi! I'm John and I'm an alcoholic." I was exposed to a level of honesty and humility that I never saw in church people. I started seeing how terribly out of touch we were in the church. We began to introduce some of these things to our ministry, and began providing help instead of harassment to those who needed it. I found a good group of our core church families had all kinds of family secrets. Growing healthy emotionally and learning how to live life on God's terms has not found much exposure in the church. I've only heard or read about a few people who have brought this concept to church. David Ferguson was the first person I met in a church setting that began to expose me to this kind of thinking. I heard, Bill Hybels of Willow Creek Community Church, share a message on the concept of emotional health through looking at three gauges. Hybels described spiritual, physical and emotional needs in that message. Saddleback Church has developed "Celebrate Recovery." Finally, in recent days, Peter Scazzero's books, *The Emotionally*

Healthy Church and his latest *Emotionally Healthy Spirituality*, has brought these issues to the table. But, for the most part this message is not understood very well in church circles. **Most church people are emotionally constipated.** Attempting to appear to be something they are not has killed much spiritual fervor in too many churchgoers. In many places, the church has become totally irrelevant because of this unwillingness to get involved in the process of "peeling the onion" of our lives.

Many of our churches have small groups of people who meet in homes. We believe these groups are the key to becoming more of what the Lord wants for us. **However, small groups are simply a tool, another method, and there is no guarantee that anything will happen in them more than has happened anywhere else with a church program.** I have heard many Christians who have given up on small groups because their experience was not productive. Groups are only as helpful as the level of honesty and safety they provide.

A lady came to see me one time and told me her family was going to look for another church. This lady was the queen of maintaining an immaculate public image. I asked why. The lady said, "We have not been able to connect here!" I asked permission to speak the truth into her life and she issued permission. I said, "It is impossible to connect with an image. You have never allowed anyone into your life. You guard your public image and all you do here is bump images with others." Until people build safety, trust and vulnerability into their relationships, little progress can be made.

Churches should be places where each of us, through our relationship with the Lord, is having our own "onion peeled," on a regular basis. Then we can share with others what is happening in our own lives. When we do, deep connections are made.

For people to begin being set free from their deep wounds of the past along with their medicating practices, **somebody has to get honest and lead the way. This is the key to any ministry's vitality.**

Through being broken, humbled and healed, I can tell my story to a group of men and within one or two nights, guys are revealing more about their woundedness than they have in years.

I recently have come on the staff of Bay Life Church, a large church in Brandon, Florida. My role is to work with the men. On the first night, I told my story as revealed here in this book. I shared how as a pastor, I medicated my pain with things that were not good. After my talk, we broke into smaller groups of men around several tables. The very first night almost every man at my table told what their battle is currently. There was a depth and vulnerability in one night that some groups never have in years. The other table leaders told me the same thing. In shock, they said their men opened up way more than the table leader expected.

People are tired of playing church. Even guys want to find some clear answers to why they do what they do. **They want to be different, they just do not know how.** They want to have the cycles broken, but need direction. They want to learn how to be better, but there has not been a safe place to tell the truth and live to tell about it. Churches have developed all kinds of support and recovery opportunities but the perception is that those groups are for the people who are really messed up. The truth is every human needs what I am communicating here, because it is the normal human experience.

The *plan* is simple; it is not simple to *practice*.

- Face your fears, uncertainties, and tragedies in life without medicating the pain.
- Instead, practice running to the Father
- Invite Him to shape you more into the image of Jesus through the experience.
- Get in a group of others who are coming to see this is the Christian human experience.
- Simply make it your focus to stay in close relationship with the Father and answer Jesus' invitation.

"Come to me, all of you who are weary and carry heavy burdens, and I will give you rest. Take my yoke upon you. Let me teach you, because I am humble and gentle, and you will find rest for your souls. For my yoke fits perfectly, and the burden I give you is light." Matthew 11:28-30

He will peel the onion one layer at a time. He will teach you and show you what needs to change. **This process will go on the rest of your life.** Why not humble yourself and jump in, cooperating fully?

As we take this adventure journey toward Christ-likeness,

health and wholeness, **it is always better to do it with some travel mates.** There are so many faulty notions in the church about what a small group of friends can do for you; I want to address that part in the next chapter.

Chapter Seventeen
SUPPORT VS. ACCOUNTABILITY

When I committed the sin that led to my dismissal, I was having a daily quiet time, preaching every Sunday and meeting with one or two pastors regularly for "accountability"! There is a common thread that runs through people who have the personality type that often leads to the stage. It can be observed in Aaron, Moses' brother. Remember Moses, requested that Aaron collaborate with him because Aaron was a better communicator than Moses? Check out the story in Exodus chapters four and thirty-two. Moses was gone for some time getting the Ten Commandments from God. He comes back and hears a sound like a battle, but instead it is a wild party. There is a golden calf set up for the Israelites to worship. When he asked Aaron where it came from, Aaron basically told Moses, We just threw a bunch of jewelry in the fire and the calf jumped out! (See Exodus 32:3 & 24)

Most people who get into ministry have a "salesman" type personality, just like Aaron. Many have a high "I" on the DISC personality profile. One of the traits of the "I" is they can be very deceptive. When not fully surrendered to the Lord, the gift to communicate can be used for self-preservation and evading the truth.

Accountability is over-rated. Here is the bottom line: **If a person is not ready, from the inside, to face their pain without medicating, no accountability group can keep them straight from the outside.**

Too many of us have learned the standard church thing. We modify our behavior in front of people who care, but do not modify it when only God is watching. Until we decide, from the depth of our person, that we want to please the Lord, even when no one else is around, then we are not ready for change. **Ultimately, it is God and me, one on one.** So, what good is a life group? What does a men's group have to offer?

The key to surrounding ourselves with a group of people is **primarily for support** while we learn a new way to live. This support happens when each person is focusing on their own walk with the Lord. When they are growing, they come to group and tell the other people what the Lord is teaching them. Only God has the power to change someone from the inside out. Colossians 2:21ff. teach us that **all the rules in the world have no effect when it comes to conquering a person's evil thoughts and desires**. A person who is committed to change from the inside out, will benefit from a group of people around him or her who can pray, support and encourage. **A person who has not committed from the inside to change will simply lie** to those who are attempting to hold him or her accountable. They may also become very evasive to any probing about themselves. Anyone who has attempted to have someone else hold them accountable has been disappointed. **It just does not work.** It sounds noble. It may give the impression of something good, but it does not work. When you have really committed to change from the inside, your accountability is to the Lord and your own internal standard.

I believe the Lord intended us to encourage each other toward godliness. The Christian life is not meant to be lived in isolation. So let's consider a couple things a support group can accomplish.

First, when you stop a pattern of medicating pain that has been part of your life for a long time, you will face **six weeks up to three months of depression.** Our groups need to know this will happen. Remember, I said each of us is a drug addict. Even if your drug is created internally, it still is created and infused into your blood stream. Removing the stimulus removes the chemical. **Removing the chemical that lifted your spirits through an adrenaline rush, puts you into withdrawal.** It takes time for your body's chemical make-up to adjust to your new pattern of behavior. Your group can encourage you, pray for you and remind you what is happening during this first phase.

Second, once the medicine is out of your system and you begin to "feel your pain," all the stuff you have been medicating and running from all your life is there to face you head on. Your life group surrounds you, and through sharing their own experience, strength and hope, you are encouraged to grow through the pain. They can help you see yourself more honestly.

Finally, once the trauma of those first six months to one year is past and you have not medicated, you will have one heck of a story to share. You will now find yourself in the ongoing "onion peel" mode. **God shows you Himself in ways you have never experienced.** He will teach you very practical and personal life lessons that you will get to share with others. There will always be struggles to face, pain to work through and new lessons to learn. Your group will be there and will be a big part of your life.

Once you are in this pattern, because you have chosen this course for yourself, you may invite someone to check on you when you know you will be facing a trying time. That type of "support" is really the only kind that has any positive effect.

Norman Geisler writes, "This is not the best possible world but the best possible way to get to the best possible world." This life is a big sifting time. Even though life will feel much better than it used to when you practice this model, we are not in heaven yet. There is always going to be some tension. We face the battle between our sinful natures, our own selfish desires, other's desires plus God's desires. We will look at that next.

Chapter Eighteen
THE TENSION

One Monday Night at the Bay Life Church Men's Meeting, I was sharing this concept when one of the newer men asked, "How good can we expect life to get?" That is a great question. That question begs for an answer. Let's wrestle with the tension of living in a crazy world yet having a strong desire to please God.

Life is complex. How good can it get? Let's look at the bad news first. The Bible is clear, there will be no end to the battle as long as we live on the planet. We have much to deal with. All the wounds from our past must be addressed and healed. All the junk we have brought upon ourselves needs to be faced and handled as biblically as possible. Then there are all the people in our lives that have not even begun on this journey. There is also a spiritual war going on and a very real enemy who wants to keep us down.

We are all deteriorating **physically** and will continue to do so until we ultimately die. **Relationally,** we will find it difficult to find another person who has done the hard work to become healthy spiritually and emotionally. Finally, the **spiritual** goal set before us is no less than to become like Jesus Christ! That makes it all seem rather impossible.

The good news is that through the Lord Jesus' death, burial and resurrection, God fully forgives and accepts us as we are. He brings us in to His family to rear us as His kids! He promises never to leave us, never to quit what He started and guarantees for each of us the task will be accomplished. He promises to be our teacher. He will correct us. He promises to use everything in life, to shape us. The Father invites us to cooperate in the process. When we stumble, He picks us up and teaches us through the stumble. He gives joy and peace on the inside for the trip. He makes reservations for us in the forever hotel!

Gayle and I marvel at how God took both our botched efforts, our failures in our marriage and the major sin on my part, and brought a diamond out of the dung. Both of us were crushed. The sin and devastation was major. **Yet, what the enemy meant to destroy us, our Father used to heal us!** Deep wounds from childhood in both of us were recognized, opened up and healed. Through His gentle direction, He walked us through a process that overwhelms us both. Thinking through what He has done for us provokes us to worship like nothing else. How the Lord does what He does is beyond us. How He can step in, take two deeply wounded people and bring growth, joy and a deeper love than ever before, is simply a "God thing."

Some may have thought our marriage was down for the count.

Six years after all the devastation, Gayle and I can say these six years have been the best of our thirty-four years together! We have learned to love life, love adventure, take risks, pray together daily, share everything and be so comfortable together, there is nowhere either of us would rather be.

How good can it get? It can get to where you can say with Paul in 2 Corinthians 4:16, "**My physical body is dying but my inner man is growing stronger every day.**" It can get so good that you look forward to getting out of bed in the morning, so good that you love life!

It has gotten where instead of being afraid someone might see a flaw in me, I invite anyone close to me to share honestly what he or she sees. I invite the Lord to peel my onion and show me what He wants to change next. Growth's benefits have been so exciting I want to keep working at it. It has become exciting to see areas I need to grow, rather than just reminding me of how inadequate I am.

Now it is more a sense the Father loves me and is gently teaching me how to be like Him. That is really all I ever wanted from my earthly father. Now I have the privilege of being taught by my Forever Father.

Jesus said that as long as you and I live in this world there will be trouble. All of us will ultimately grow sick and die. Some may die tragically. The good news is that does not change anything but your address! I want to talk about the "continuation of the journey" in the last chapter.

Chapter Nineteen
COMMENCEMENT

One of the things Gayle and I began to notice as we healed was that a life without adventure equals a lack of passion. We began a practice I would highly recommend. On days off, we would hold hands, pray, and ask the Father to give us what we needed. We asked Him to lead us and help us see His hand through out our adventure. Then we would take off in the car with no plan, just a faith that the Father delights in us! Oh, it would take another book to tell you the stories of times everything came together to give us a day off no travel agent could have planned. So many times the Father's smile upon us was so obvious it moved us to awe.

The thing that became most obvious to us is the Father created us for adventure and for discovery and He delights in us. To drive into a small town that we had never seen before, meant every turn was adventure. We never knew what was around the next corner. It became clear to us that having a trip on the calendar was equally important. Just knowing another adventure was coming next week lifted our spirits.

Do you realize the Father hard-wired all of us that way? Why do you think Jesus promised He was going to prepare a place for us? Why do you think His return and the prospects of heaven have captured Christians for centuries? It is because He knew we lived life more fully when we know something good is coming.

Many in the church have neutered Heaven. I have heard too many people ask, what are we going to do up there? Won't it be boring?

I believe God is infinite; there is no end to the depth of His person. I believe the Scriptures teach that heaven or eternity will be an "**unfolding of ages.**" It will not be some boring, static, ho-hum, I have seen it all, now what, kind of place. It will not be like going to Disney and being excited for the three days it takes to see it all!

Heaven is going to be an adventure that takes **forever to unfold.** It will be like going to one new place after another. It will be like meeting the most interesting, fascinating people imaginable and new ones every day, and never having enough time to hear all they have to share. It will be a constant learning of the greatness and wonder of the Father, Son and Spirit, without ever being able to comprehend or know it all. It will be the most adventurous, stimulating, mind expanding, heart exploding, and awe inspiring journey and place for us. The future the Father has planned for us has no equal.

I believe when we really begin connecting the dots in this life, we experience the beginning of what heaven will be like. Because so many good things happen to us on the inside, going to heaven will be a very expansive continuation of what God has begun in us here.

Conclusion

So, I am sitting in my hotel room in Palm Beach County, Florida. I'm traveling for my work. I have two nights here, three hours from home. There are no more than a dozen people who know me from West Palm Beach to Vero Beach. I have a TV in my room with HBO. I have a laptop connected to wireless, high-speed Internet, with no filters and I have every imaginable escape available to me within an hour's drive. I am learning separation from the Lord is purely internal. In our world, there is nowhere I can go to remove myself from all temptation or opportunity to sin.

There was a time in my life that the combination of being alone with all this opportunity would have meant a huge internal struggle and ultimately a defeat. I could never win a battle when in an environment like that. In fact, the only time I won was when I did not have a chance to fail. It was terrible to be alone. The war raged and my mind always switched to the pleasure. I could have told three accountability partners to grill me when I got home. I could have had the strongest commitment not to fold. When I got away and was alone, the deep woundedness in me surfaced. The pain of being alone, with no noise and no public image to maintain, had my mind racing for relief.

There are three great indicators of our deep wounds healing; **three litmus tests to see if we are growing in spiritual and emotional health.** First, when I am alone do I act differently than I would if my wife or my pastor were right beside me? Second, the quality and depth of my personal relationships is a thermometer revealing my health. Finally, am I able to face the struggles of life without medicating the pain?

Return to my hotel room. I start my day at 5:00 a.m., just as if I was home. I have a forty-five minute quiet time of reading the Bible and prayer. After that I head out and run for forty-five minutes. On my run, I remind myself what I want most in life. I desire intimacy with God, intimacy with Gayle, and now, impact on other guys. I pledge another twenty-four hours of saying, "Yes" to God and "No" to lesser things. I clean up, eat and go to work for the day. Usually, through the course of a day, I see my reflection in another person that reveals some flaws in me that need attention. At the end of the workday, I enjoy a nice meal in a restaurant by myself. It is strange, I am alone but not lonely. I feel at peace in my own skin. There is no harsh battle raging. There may be an occasional stray thought but it succumbs rather quickly. I usually think of what I would order Gayle if she were with me. I have a Blackberry and send an email to Gayle telling her what I am eating, and what I would get for her if she were with me. I really enjoy seeing couples, families and some lonely looking businessmen. I am thankful! I head back to my room, make a few phone calls and watch some TV. Call Gayle and we have our prayer time over the telephone, and I go to bed. I sleep like a baby and do it all over again.

I feel no compulsion to fix or control anybody else, but I do have a big compassion to help fellow strugglers. I have a steady stream of people who are seeking me out to get help with their lives. I know I create a safe and peaceful setting for many to get honest for the first time. It is a benefit of the healing God has allowed me to experience. I regularly share with others the life lessons I'm learning currently, no matter how humbling they may be.

I can do whatever I choose to do. I can become whatever I choose to become. I am choosing to face whatever life has for me without medicating. I am learning the Great Physician dispenses the only medicine I need. I am learning to run to Him. Through connecting the dots in my life and facing the pain head on, I've found peace.

"So take a new grip with your tired hands and stand firm on your shaky legs. Mark out a straight path for your feet. Then those who follow you, though they are weak and lame, will not stumble and fall but will become strong." Hebrews 12:12-13

Appendix A
My Dad

Everyone has their own story that shapes how they live. My dad was a loyal man. He worked the same job his entire adult life. He was married to my mom and they stuck together, through thick and thin, for forty-two years. Dad died at sixty-five years old, and I had the honor of preaching his funeral. He was a WWII veteran and a POW. I can't imagine the trauma of being a nineteen to twenty year-old held captive in Rumania after being shot out of the sky and parachuting from five miles up.

Dad was physically present, but seemed emotionally absent from me during my boyhood days. My sister would tell a very different story. Dad was very active with her, teaching her many things about life. That was the kind of relationship I experienced with my mom, but not Dad.

When I married and moved away from home to go to Bible College, I wrote Dad a letter and shared the distance I had always felt. He responded very positively and we had at least ten great years together before he died. We went on vacations together, golfed, fished, crabbed at the ocean, played "world champion" card games, and had some very deep discussions about life. Dad was very active with my children. In fact, one Fathers' Day Sunday, the Lord showed me that the way my dad treated my son was the way he would treat me, if he could do it over again. Everyone in the family knew how close Grandpa and "Bucko" were. Grandchildren are a second chance for parents.

The last thing I want to do in this writing is to dishonor my dad. I have come to see that his consistency at home and his very presence made a difference in my life. I am extremely grateful for those last ten years, the memories, the bear hugs and the development of a great relationship.

Caring for my dad at home when he was dying, and then being the one to speak at his funeral are honors I cherish to this day.

Appendix B
REVIEW

Each Chapter in One Sentence

1. You are born with many physical, emotional and spiritual needs that are universal.
2. When those needs are not met, it creates pain.
3. You are born with a bent toward self-centeredness and self will.
4. Wrong choices create pain.
5. Life is filled with all kinds of hurt and pain
6. The normal human response to pain is to "medicate" that pain.
7. There are many kinds of pain in life, some very subtle.
8. Some of the pain we experience is brutal.
9. Unhealthy ways of medicating pain cause us to develop a public image and private self that are quite different.

10. There is no quick fix, pill or silver bullet to solve our dilemma.

11. We may choose to humble ourselves before we are humiliated.

12. Learning to surrender ourselves fully to the Lord is a powerful tool.

13. Facing pain and running to the Father is the key concept in this book.

14. Sometimes it just takes divine intervention to heal some of the old, deep wounds we carry.

15. The power to receive forgiveness from God, then extend it to others and finally to ourselves is major in the search for peace.

16. Now that we feel safe, we invite God to continue to peel the layers of our lives for more growth to happen.

17. People to come around you, support, and encourage you on this journey are of more importance than thinking someone else can create your change for you.

18. As long as we are living on earth, there will be a tension between living fully for God and folding to the pressures all around us.

19. A glimpse into what I perceive eternity will be like.

20. Conclusion. What life looks like for me currently.

CPSIA information can be obtained at www.ICGtesting.com
Printed in the USA
240666LV00001B/7/P

9 781424 177561